T0084330

Johan Svendsen (1840 – 1911)
Romanze

Romance

for Violin and Orchestra
für Violine und Orchester
pour violon et orchestre

opus 26

Arranged by | Bearbeitet von | Arrangée par
Wilhelm Lutz

Edited, with Preface and Teaching Notes by
Herausgegeben mit einem Vorwort und Hinweisen für den Unterricht von
Éditée, avec préface et indications pour l'apprentissage par
Annette Seyfried

Piano Reduction | Klavierauszug

Level | Schwierigkeitsgrad D/USA: 3 UK/AUS: 6

SE 1044
ISMN 979-0-001-16730-7

▶ **MP3 play-along separately available:**
www.schott-student-edition.com

www.schott-music.com

Mainz · London · Berlin · Madrid · New York · Paris · Prague · Tokyo · Toronto
© 2019 SCHOTT MUSIC GmbH & Co. KG, Mainz · Printed in Germany

Preface

In the nineteenth Century Johan Severin Svendsen (1840–1911) embarked on a career as yet unparalleled for a Scandinavian musician. Having made a favourable impression on the Norwegian-Swedish Consul while on tour, Svendsen was awarded a royal bursary enabling him to travel to Leipzig to study with established figures including Ferdinand David (violin), Reinecke, Hauptmann and Richter (composition). Problems with his left hand obliged Svendsen to relinquish his initial goal of becoming a virtuoso violinist, but after his years of training many opportunities arose, including a study tour with the publisher Brockhaus, concerts in Paris with Saint-Saëns and guest performances in Weimar. He performed as a violinist at the first Bayreuth Festival in 1872 (indeed, Wagner became godfather to Svendsen's Jewish wife). Together with Edvard Grieg, Svendsen directed the royal symphonic concert series in Norway from 1872–1874, an outstanding achievement in his homeland. From 1872–1883 he conducted the music society concerts in Christiania (apart from three years spent abroad) and in 1883 he was appointed conductor at the royal Opera in Copenhagen, where he spent the rest of his life.

Svendsen was rightly identified by his contemporaries as an international Romantic. Grieg wrote of him in admiration: 'He has everything that I myself lack …', with a natural gift for instrumentation and unforced mastery of classical form. His ties with Norway are strong and many Norwegian cultural echoes feature in his compositions – as in this Romance for violin and orchestra op. 26 in G major, which he composed in just two days in 1881. At the time Svendsen had no idea that this would become his most celebrated work.

This Romance is a musical gem with a great range of emotion and imagery offering all sorts of opportunities for creative interpretation. It is based on ABA form: the gentle, richly coloured first section gives way to a dance-like middle section that also begins *piano*, but which builds up *molto animato* to an ecstatic *fortissimo* before the opening theme reappears in subtly varied guise. The piece then dwindles away almost to nothing.

Annette Seyfried
Translation Julia Rushworth

Vorwort

Johan Joachim Svendsen (1840–1911) startete im 19. Jahrhundert eine bislang beispiellose Karriere für einen skandinavischen Musiker. Mit einem königlichen Stipendium in der Tasche – er beeindruckte auf einer Tournee den norwegisch-schwedischen Konsul – reiste er nach Leipzig, um dort bei namhaften Persönlichkeiten wie Ferdinand David (Violine), Reinecke, Hauptmann und Richter (Komposition) zu studieren. Sein Ziel war zunächst Violinvirtuose zu werden, was er durch Krämpfe in der linken Hand zurückstellen musste. Nach seiner Ausbildung ergaben sich vielfältige Möglichkeiten, wie zum Beispiel eine Studienreise mit dem Verleger Brockhaus, Konzerte in Paris mit Saint-Saëns, Gastspiele in Weimar. Er spielte als Geiger bei den ersten Bayreuther Festspiele 1872. (Wagner war Taufpate seiner jüdischen Frau.) Sevendsen leitete gemeinsam mit Eduard Grieg von 1872–1874 die königlichen Sinfoniekonzerte in Norwegen, ein Höhepunkt bislang in seinem Land. Von 1872–1883 war er mit dreijähriger Unterbrechung Dirigent der Musikvereinskonzerte in Kristiania und wurde 1883 zum Dirigenten der königlichen Oper in Kopenhagen ernannt, wo er den Rest seines Lebens verbrachte.

Svendsen wird zurecht von seinen Zeitgenossen der internationalen Romantik zugeordnet. Sein Bewunderer Grieg schrieb über ihn: „Er hat all das, was ich nicht habe …", eine natürliche Begabung zur Instrumentation und eine selbstverständliche Beherrschung der klassischen Form. Auch ist seine Verbundenheit zu Norwegen nicht zu verleugnen und man findet in seinen Kompositionen viele norwegische Anregungen. So auch in der hier vorliegenden Romanze für Violine und Orchester op. 26 in G-Dur, die er 1881 in nur zwei Tagen komponierte. Damals ahnte er noch nicht, dass dies sein berühmtestes Werk werden würde.

Die Romanze ist ein musikalisches Kleinod mit unterschiedlichsten Stimmungen und Bildern und bietet vielfältigste Gestaltungsmöglichkeiten. Ihr liegt die Form ABA zugrunde. Der farbenreiche zarte ruhige 1. Teil wird durch einen tänzerischen Mittelteil unterbrochen, der ebenfalls im *piano* beginnt, sich aber bis zur Ekstase im *fortissimo* in einem *molto animato* hochschraubt, bevor das leicht variierte Anfangsthema wiederkehrt. Das Stück entschwindet quasi im Nichts.

Annette Seyfried

Préface

Johan Joachim Svendsen (1840–1911) mena au 19e siècle une carrière exemplaire pour un musicien scandinave. Bourse royale en poche – lors d'une tournée, ses prestations avaient impressionné le consul norvégo-suédois –, il se rendit à Leipzig afin de s'y former auprès de personnalités renommées du monde musical telles que Ferdinand David (violon), Reinecke, Hauptmann et Richter (composition), avec pour objectif initial de devenir violoniste virtuose. Mais des crampes à la main gauche l'obligèrent à revoir son projet. Après sa formation s'ouvrirent à lui de nombreuses opportunités, dont en particulier un voyage d'étude avec l'éditeur Brockhaus, des concerts à Paris avec Saint-Saëns et d'autres à Weimar. En 1872, il participa au premier festival de Bayreuth en tant que violoniste (Wagner était le parrain de sa femme qui était de confession juive). De 1872 à 1874, conjointement avec Edvard Grieg, Svendsen dirigea les concerts symphoniques royaux de Norvège qui constituaient alors le point culminant de l'univers musical dans son pays. De 1872 à 1883, avec trois ans d'interruption, il dirigea les concerts de la société de musique de Christiana et fut nommé en 1883 chef de l'opéra royal de Copenhague où il passa le reste de sa vie.

Ses contemporains classaient Svendsen parmi les représentants du romantisme international, à juste titre. Fervent admirateur, Grieg écrivit un jour à son propos : « Il a tout ce que je n'ai pas … », un don naturel pour l'instrumentation et une maîtrise évidente de la forme classique. Son lien à la Norvège est également indéniable tant ses compositions foisonnent d'éléments d'inspiration norvégienne. C'est aussi le cas de la romance pour violon et orchestre op. 26 en *sol* majeur présentée ici, qu'il composa en 1881 en seulement deux jours. Il était alors loin de se douter qu'elle deviendrait son œuvre la plus célèbre.

La romance est un petit bijou musical aux atmosphères et tableaux très variés dont les possibilités d'interprétation sont innombrables. Elle repose sur la forme ABA. La première partie délicate et calme est interrompue par une partie centrale dansante qui commence également *piano* puis s'exacerbe progressivement jusqu'au *fortissimo* dans un mouvement *molto animato* avant le retour du thème initial légèrement modifié. Pour finir, la pièce semble s'évanouir dans le néant.

Annette Seyfried
Traduction Michaëla Rubi

Romance / Romanze

Johan S. Svendsen
1840–1911
Piano Arr.: Wilhelm Lutz

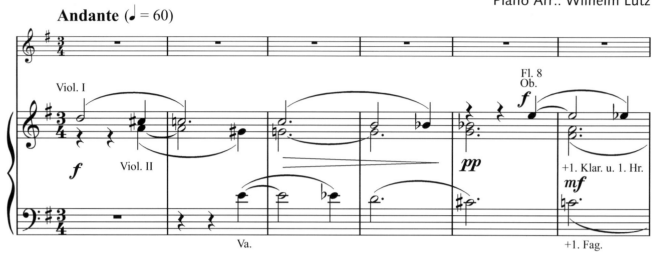

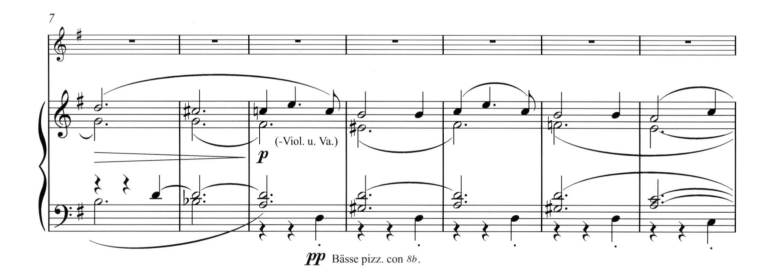

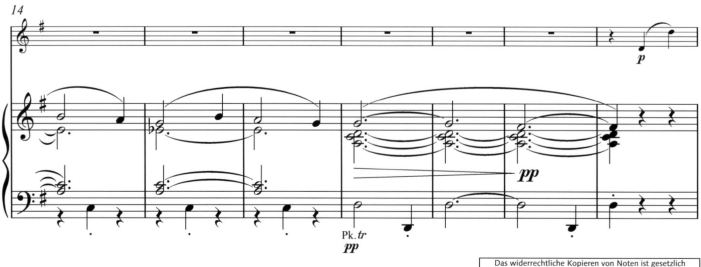

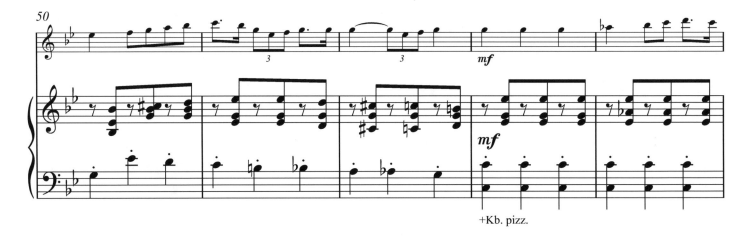

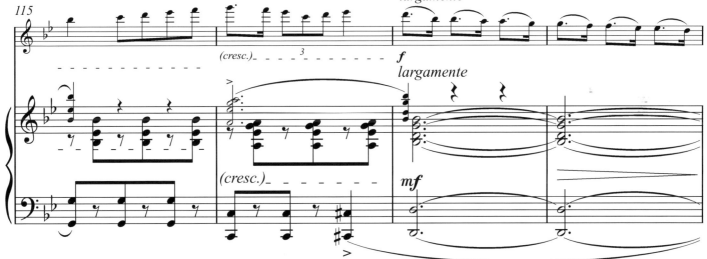

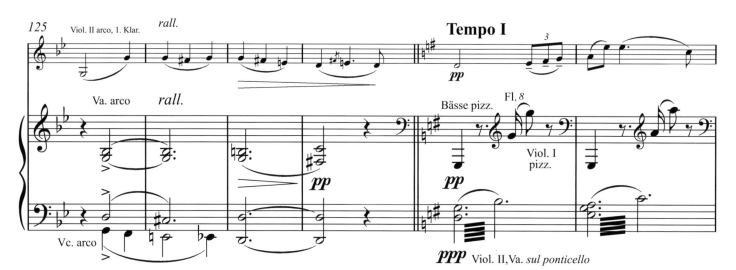

4

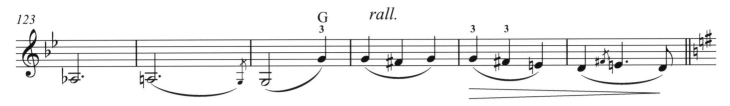

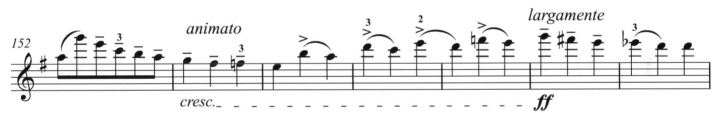

Romance / Romanze

Johan S. Svendsen
1840–1911

Johan Svendsen (1840 – 1911)
Romanze

Romance

for Violin and Orchestra
für Violine und Orchester
pour violon et orchestre

opus 26

Arranged by | Bearbeitet von | Arrangée par
Wilhelm Lutz

Edited, with Preface and Teaching Notes by
Herausgegeben mit einem Vorwort und Hinweisen für den Unterricht von
Éditée, avec préface et indications pour l'apprentissage par
Annette Seyfried

Piano Reduction | Klavierauszug

Level | Schwierigkeitsgrad D/USA: 3 UK/AUS: 6

SE 1044
ISMN 979-0-001-16730-7

Violin | Violine | Violon

▶ **MP3 play-along separately available:**
www.schott-student-edition.com

www.schott-music.com

Mainz · London · Berlin · Madrid · New York · Paris · Prague · Tokyo · Toronto
© 2019 SCHOTT MUSIC GmbH & Co. KG, Mainz · Printed in Germany

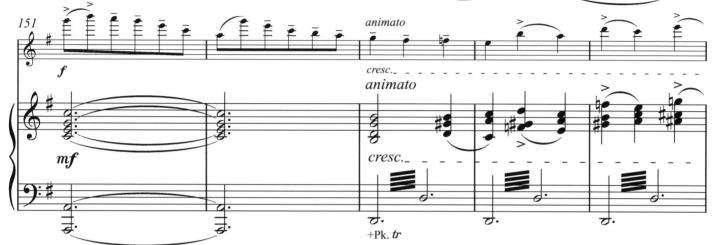

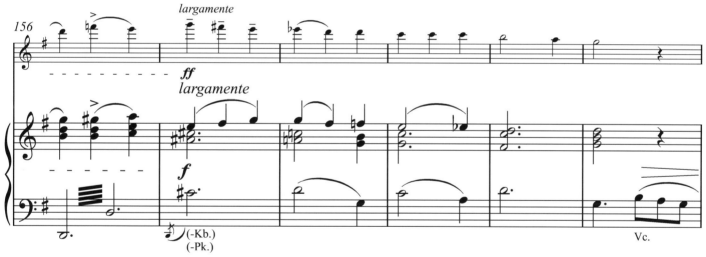

12

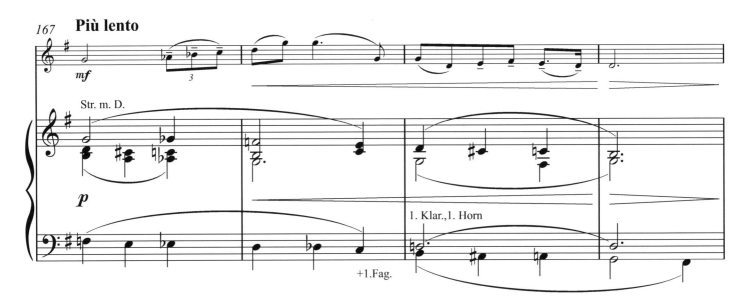

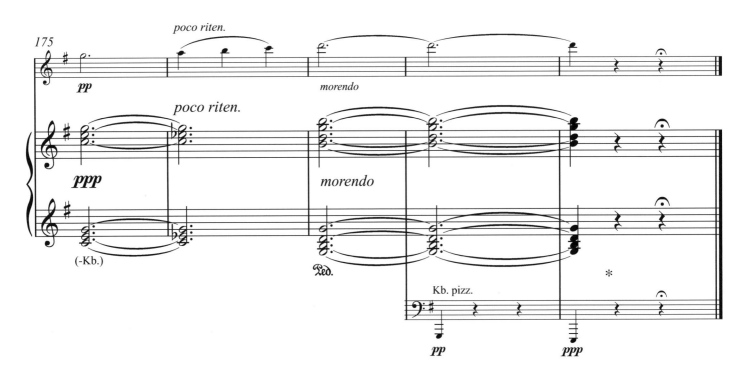

Teaching Notes

In order to understand this Romance with its broad range of motifs, melodies and phrases, a little formal analysis is recommended as a basis for developing an imaginative interpretation of its various sections. What do I aim to express as a musician and performer, what emotions would I like to draw out? What moods do I wish to evoke – and at what points? This music ranges from tender to ecstatic, from quiet calm to livelier movement in the dance-like middle section.

What techniques are required to give expression to this composition? What techniques will I need to master to give this piece colourful phrasing? Bold and simple examples are presented here with preliminary exercises as an introduction to tackling individual challenges.

A. Technical challenges for the right hand

This Romance calls for highly developed bowing technique. Knowing how to use the right part of the bow, adjust the point of contact with the string, bowing speed and weight applied – all these skills are required for creating phrases with a sense of direction. Seamless bow changes and string crossings are needed to produce a lovely *legato* effect that 'sings' on the violin. To achieve lightness of tone, individual notes have to be shaped and rounded in sound, especially in the dance-like middle section. Bringing life to a phrase requires the ability to develop or relax tone quality on a single note. It can often be observed that *piano* sounds lack resonance, with *forte* sounding forced, thin tone in high positions, breaks in *legato* with position changes, gaps in sound in phrases that include string crossing and bow changes, notes ending abruptly.

How can I overcome these deficiencies?

Below is a list of challenges for the right hand with a relevant example that can be applied to similar passages.

Dynamics:

• *piano*

The piece begins with a *piano* phrase to be played very tenderly.

To achieve lightness of tone and a sense of direction, the bow should move as fast as possible; in particular, avoid slowing down or stopping before changing bow. Playing the bowing pattern on one note first is recommended, until good tone is produced at the right point of contact with the string, with seamless bow changes. Using fast bow speed to play *piano*, the right point of contact will be closer to the fingerboard.

Preliminary exercise:

If the aim is to play everything with whole bows, then quarter notes (crotchets) must be played lighter than half notes (minims) to avoid producing an accent with increased bow speed.

With practice on a single note it is helpful to imagine the pattern of notes first, before actually playing.

• *forte*

Here the same pattern can be followed as for a lovely *piano* tone: play through the bowing pattern *forte* on a single note until a gleaming sound emerges.

This time the point of contact is close to the bridge, while still allowing lovely tone production with plenty of bow.

How does the left hand influence the sound here? The very first note takes me into a high position, so I have to start very close to the bridge and then move away from it a little, bowing slightly away from me.

• *crescendo – decrescendo*

There are several ways of varying dynamics: adjusting the point of contact, bow speed and weight applied to the bow – usually all three of these have a part to play.

In order to play *piano* at the beginning very lightly, using plenty of bow, for the *crescendo* I must adapt the point of contact and weight of bow. That involves moving towards the bridge and using greater arm weight. For a *decrescendo*, the opposite applies. To avoid producing unwanted noises when shifting the point of contact with the string, the bow should not be held straight across the string, but moved at a slight angle: this means drawing the hand forward on a down bow and angling it away on an up bow, moving towards the bridge and then back towards the fingerboard. In this instance I aim to achieve a *crescendo* on the up bow by moving the bow inward, coming closer to the bridge for increased sound and for playing in high positions. For *decrescendo* I use a slightly angled bow stroke to move away from the bridge again.

Bowing styles:

• *legato*
Playing a lovely *legato* requires steady bow speed – and this involves planning ahead. What length of bow do I have available for each note, so that my tone doesn't sound thin?

Here the bow must be divided into thirds: this means moving the bow more slowly than in the preceding bar and playing very close to the bridge. For the *decrescendo*, gradually reduce the weight of bow applied.

• *portato*
With *portato* it is important that the bow does not stop. The individual note is shaped by adjusting the weight applied and speed of movement, like a little pendulum.

Another consideration is creating a sense of movement towards the third beat, using less bow for the first note than for the second, with the third note using more than either.

• 'Bell sounds'
Bell sounds have an opening and closing phase, as with a pendulum. Using plenty of bow will produce a lighter and livelier sound, suitable for the dance-like middle section.

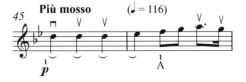

• Seamless string crossings
In order to achieve seamless string crossings, the next string should be approached gradually, not with a sudden jolt. Awareness has to be developed of when the movement across to the next string should begin in order to reach it at precisely the right time.

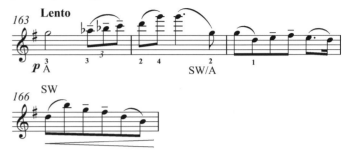

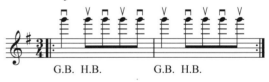

• Tone quality in high positions
When playing in higher positions, the bow must move correspondingly closer to the bridge. Here again it will be useful to find the right kind of sound with the appropriate bowing pattern on a single note for practice. In high positions on the E string the weight of the bow will have to be rationed so the note does not 'squeal'.

Preliminary exercise:

B. Technical challenges for the left hand

The left hand has an important contribution to make in shaping this piece with appropriate colours, using different strings for different tone qualities. Numerous position changes and finger extensions will be required. In many places *glissandi* are possible. Maintaining accurate intonation through many harmonic and key changes is a challenge. It is important to be aware of the fingering patterns used: where do the semitones lie, which fingers are close together and which further apart?
Furthermore, the use of variable vibrato is essential.

As this piece requires all kinds of position changes, here I would just like to explain the difference between a complete change in position and the technique of using extensions, with examples. Confusion here is very frequently at the root of mistakes.
Anyone wishing to examine the subject of position changes in more detail may like to consult Schott's series of books on systematic violin technique, ED 21162–21164.

With a position change the entire hand shifts into the new position; when playing *legato*, this process is audible. With extensions, only one finger reaches up or down into the new position, sometimes followed by the whole hand shifting into that new position: here no other notes are heard in between. The choice between these types of shift will generally be made for musical reasons, depending on the desired effect (though sometimes the size of a player's own hand will also be a determining factor). In any case, it is important to distinguish between these two types of shift and decide which to use, in order to achieve accuracy and good intonation.

The technique of using extensions plays a significant role in this piece, yet little systematic explanation or practice is generally offered. For this reason I'd like to present two examples of this technique with preliminary exercises as a clear and simple introduction.

Example 1: upward extension

Preliminary exercise:

Example 2: downward extension

Preliminary exercise:

The hand remains in position in both instances in these exercises.

Annette Seyfried
Translation Julia Rushworth

Hinweise für den Unterricht

Um die Romanze mit ihren vielfältigen Motiven, Melodien, Phrasen zu erfassen, empfiehlt es sich zunächst, eine kleine Formanalyse zu machen und eine Idee, eine Vorstellung zu den verschiedenen Abschnitten zu entwickeln. Was möchte ich als Musiker/Interpret sagen, welche Empfindungen möchte ich hervorrufen? Welche Stimmungen möchte ich wo wecken? Die Bandbreite liegt hier zwischen einer *gewissen* Zartheit bis hin zur Ekstase, zwischen Stille und Ruhe bis hin zu einer schwungvollen Bewegung im tänzerischen Mittelteil.

Welche technischen Mittel sind notwendig, um diese Aussagen zu transportieren? Was muss ich beherrschen, um das Stück farbenreich zu gestalten? An plakativen Beispielen möchte ich hier mit Vorübungen die einzelnen Herausforderungen vorstellen.

A. Technische Herausforderungen für die rechte Hand

Die Romanze stellt hohe Anforderungen an die Bogentechnik. Ein gutes Gefühl für Bogeneinteilung, für Kontaktstelle, Bogengeschwindigkeit und Bogengewicht wird verlangt, um Phrasen zu bilden und diesen Richtung zu geben. Dichte Bogenwechsel und Saitenwechsel sind notwendig, um ein schönes *legato* zu erzeugen und damit auf der Geige zu „singen". Für eine Leichtigkeit im Klang ist es wichtig, einzelne Töne mit einer Ein- und Ausschwingphase zu formen, insbesondere im tänzerischen Mittelteil. Um eine Phrase lebendig werden zu lassen, muss ich Klang auf einem einzigen Ton entwickeln oder auch entspannen können.

Häufig stellt man fest: das *piano* klingt nicht, das *forte* ist gedrückt, ich habe keinen Klang in hohen Lagen, kein *legato* bei Lagenwechseln, Klanglöcher entstehen in Phrasen bei Saiten- und Bogenwechsel, der Ton endet abrupt. Wie kann ich das beheben?

Nachfolgend eine kleine Liste mit den Anforderungen für die rechte Hand und ein entsprechendes Beispiel, was auf ähnliche Stellen übertragen werden kann.

Dynamik:

• *piano*

Das Stück beginnt mit einer Phrase im *piano*, die sehr zart zu spielen ist.

Um eine Leichtigkeit im Klang und auch Richtung zu erzeugen, brauche ich eine möglichst hohe Bogengeschwindigkeit, insbesondere vor dem Bogenwechsel darf ich nicht bremsen oder gar stehenbleiben. Es empfiehlt sich, das Bogenschema zunächst auf einem Ton zu spielen, bis der gewünschten Klang an der passenden Kontaktstelle mit dichtem Bogenwechsel erreicht ist. Bei hoher Bogengeschwindigkeit und *piano* befindet sich die geeignete Kontaktstelle näher am Griffbrett.

Wenn ich alles mit G.B. spielen möchte, muss ich die Viertelnoten noch leichter als die halben Noten spielen, um nicht immer eine Betonung durch die höhere Bogengeschwindigkeit zu bekommen.

Beim Üben auf einem Ton ist es hilfreich, sich den Notentext innerlich vorzustellen, bevor man ihn dann tatsächlich spielt.

• *forte*

Hier kann man das gleiche Muster anwenden wie für einen schönen *piano*-Klang: Auf einem Ton das Bogenschema nun im *forte* üben, bis ein strahlender Klang entsteht.

Diesmal ist die Kontaktstelle am Steg, aber nur so weit, dass ich noch einen schönen Klang mit viel Bogen erzeugen kann.

Welche Parameter kommen durch die linke Hand hinzu? Ich befinde mich zunächst mit dem 1. Ton in einer hohen Lage, also muss ich sehr nah am Steg starten und mich dann etwas entfernen. Das bedeutet, ich muss etwas nach hinten streichen.

• *crescendo – decrescendo*
Um die Dynamik zu ändern, habe ich mehrere Möglichkeiten. Ich kann die Kontaktstelle verändern, die Bogengeschwindigkeit und das Bogengewicht. Meist spielen alle drei Parameter eine Rolle.

Da ich das *piano* hier zu Beginn mit einer Leichtigkeit spielen möchte, also mit viel Bogen schon starte, muss ich für das *crescendo* die Kontaktstelle und das Bogengewicht verändern. Das bedeutet, ich muss mich zum Steg mit mehr Armgewicht bewegen. Im *decrescendo* passiert das Gegenteil. Um keine unschönen Geräusche beim Kontaktstellenwechsel zu erzeugen, darf ich nicht den Bogen parallel verschieben, sondern muss dies durch leichtes Schrägstreichen erzielen. Das bedeutet, im Abstrich nach vorne zu streichen und im Aufstrich nach hinten, um mich zum Steg zu bewegen, und umgekehrt, um wieder Richtung Griffbrett zu kommen. In diesem Fall möchte ich insbesondere den Aufstrich crescendieren, indem ich nach innen streiche. Dadurch komme ich näher zum Steg für mehr Klang und das Spiel in hohen Lagen. Für das *decrescendo* verwende ich ebenso einen leichten Schrägstrich, um mich wieder weg vom Steg zu bewegen.

Stricharten:

• *legato*
Für ein schönes *legato* brauche ich eine gleichmäßige Bogengeschwindigkeit. Auch hier muss man vorausplanen. Wie viel Bogen habe ich für jeden Ton zur Verfügung, damit mein Klang nicht „verhungert"?

Hier muss ich den Bogen genau dritteln. Das bedeutet, der Bogen ist sofort langsamer als im Takt vorher zu ziehen und es ist direkt am Steg zu spielen. Für das *decrescendo* muss man nach und nach das Bogengewicht reduzieren.

• *portato*
Beim *portato* ist es wichtig, dass der Bogen nicht stoppt. Ich forme den einzelnen Ton nur durch Gewichts- und Geschwindigkeitsveränderung wie bei einem kleinen Pendel.

Hier kommt noch hinzu, dass ich der Zählzeit 3 Richtung geben möchte, das heißt, der erste Ton hat weniger Bogen als der zweite, der dritte am meisten.

- „Glockentöne"

Glockentöne haben eine Ein- und Ausschwingphase, wie bei einem Pendel. Verwende ich viel Bogen entsteht dabei eine gewisse Leichtigkeit, bzw. Lebendigkeit, die ich gerne im tänzerischen Mittelteil erzielen möchte.

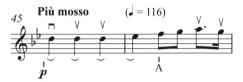

- Dichte Saitenwechsel

Um einen dichten Saitenwechsel zu erzielen, muss ich mich langsam der nächsten Saite nähern, nicht ruckartig. Dazu muss ich ein Gefühl entwickeln, wann ich mit der Saitenwechselbewegung beginnen muss, um rechtzeitig auf die neue Saite zu kommen.

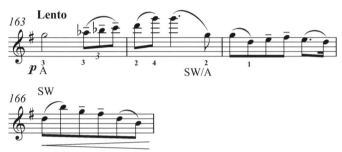

- Klang in hohen Lagen

Je höher ich in den Lagen spiele, umso näher muss sich der Bogen zum Steg bewegen. Auch hier ist es hilfreich, einen Klang mit dem entsprechenden Bogenschema auf einem Ton zu suchen und zu üben. In hohen Lagen auf der E-Saite muss man das Bogengewicht wohl dosieren, damit der Ton nicht „schreit".

Vorübung:

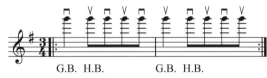

B. Technische Herausforderungen für die linke Hand

Um dieses Stück farbenreich zu gestalten und die verschieden Saiten als Klangfarbe nutzen zu können, ist auch die linke Hand sehr gefordert. Es sind viele Lagenwechsel bzw. auch die Technik des Ablangens notwendig. An manchen Stellen sind *glissandi* möglich. Durch viele Harmonie- und Tonartwechsel ist die Intonation eine Herausforde-

rung. Man muss sich immer wieder die Griffart, in der man sich gerade befindet, klar machen: Wo liegen meine Halbtöne, welche Finger sind eng gegriffen, welche weit? Darüber hinaus ist der Gebrauch eines variablen Vibratos essentiell.

Da dieses Stück alle Arten von Lagenwechseln voraussetzt, möchte ich hier nur auf den Unterschied zwischen einem vollständigen Lagenwechsel und der Technik des Ablangens mit Beispielen eingehen. Hier entstehen die häufigsten Fehlerquellen.
Wer sich umfassender mit dem Thema Lagenwechsel beschäftigen möchte, dem sei die *Systematische Violintechnik* (Schott ED 21162–21164) empfohlen.

Ein Lagenwechsel bedeutet: die ganze Hand rutscht in die neue Lage. Man hört im *legato* diesen Prozess. Beim Ablangen streckt man nur den neuen Finger nach oben oder unten in die neue Lage ab und rutscht im nächsten Schritt dann gegebenenfalls in die neue Lage mit der kompletten Hand. Somit hört man keine Zwischentöne. Man entscheidet bei der Wahl der Bewegung meist aus musikalischer Sicht, was man hören möchte. (Manchmal muss man auch die Möglichkeiten der eigenen Handgröße berücksichtigen.) Es ist in jedem Fall wichtig, sich den Unterschied in der Bewegung klar zu machen und zu entscheiden, welche man ausführen möchte, um eine Treffsicherheit und damit eine gute Intonation zu erreichen.

Die Technik des Ablangens spielt in diesem Stück eine große Rolle, wird meist aber nicht systematisch eingeführt und geübt. Aus diesem Grund möchte ich hier an zwei Beispielen mit Vorübungen diese Technik erklären und plakativ vorstellen.

Beispiel 1: Ablangen nach oben

Vorübung:

Beispiel 2: Ablangen nach unten

Vorübung:

Die Hand bleibt jeweils in der Lage bei diesen Übungen.

Annette Seyfried

Indications pour l'apprentissage

Afin d'appréhender la romance et sa grande variété de motifs, de mélodies et de phrases, il recommandé d'effectuer tout d'abord une petite analyse formelle et de développer sa propre idée, sa représentation des différents passages. En tant que musicien/interprète, qu'ai-je envie d'exprimer, quels sentiments ai-envie d'évoquer ? Quelles atmosphères ai-je envie de créer ? L'éventail s'étend ici d'une certaine délicatesse jusqu'à l'extase, du calme et de la sérénité au mouvement animé plein d'élan et dansant de la partie centrale.

Quels sont les moyens techniques nécessaires à la mise en œuvre de ces intentions ? Quels éléments dois-je maîtriser afin d'interpréter ce morceau de manière vivante et colorée ? Je voudrais ici présenter les différentes exigences techniques à l'aide d'exemples clairs et explicites.

A. Exigences techniques pour la main droite

La romance est très exigeante du point de vue de la technique d'archet. Une bonne maîtrise de la répartition de l'archet, de son point de contact, de sa vitesse et de son poids sont nécessaires pour permettre de construire les phrases et leur donner une direction. De même, la densité des changements de cordes et d'archet l'est afin de créer un beau *legato* et faire « chanter » le violon. Pour la légèreté du son, il est important de former chaque son individuellement avec une phase d'attaque et d'extinction, en particulier dans la partie centrale. Afin de donner vie à une phrase, je dois être capable de développer le son puis de le relâcher sur chaque note.
Constat fréquent : le *piano* ne sonne pas, le *forte* est tendu, je n'ai pas de son dans les positions hautes, pas de *legato* au changement de positions, des trous sonores se créent dans les phrases nécessitant des changements de corde ou d'archet, le son s'arrête abruptement.
Comment remédier à ces difficultés ?
Vous trouverez ci-dessous une petite liste des exigences correspondant à la main droite assorties d'exemples de solutions pouvant être appliquées aux passages similaires.

Dynamique :

• *piano*
La pièce commence *piano* par une phrase devant être jouée avec beaucoup de délicatesse.

Afin de donner de la légèreté au son et de lui conférer une direction, j'ai besoin de la vitesse d'archet la plus grande possible, sans freiner ni m'arrêter avant le changement d'archet. Il est recommandé de s'entraîner d'abord à exécuter les enchaînements de l'archet sur une seule note jusqu'à obtenir le son souhaité au point de contact adéquat et avec la densité requise. Pour un jeu *piano* avec une grande vitesse d'archet, le point de contact se trouve plus près de la touche.

Si je veux tout jouer avec tout l'archet, les noires seront plus légères que les blanches afin d'éviter une accentuation systématique liée à une plus grande vitesse d'archet.
Lorsqu'on travaille sur une note, il est utile de se représenter intérieurement ce que l'on va jouer au préalable.

• *forte*

Il est possible de procéder ici de la même manière que pour un joli son *piano* : travailler la répartition de l'archet sur une seule note jusqu'à obtenir un son rayonnant.

Cette fois, le point de contact est au chevalet, mais seulement aussi longtemps qu'il est encore possible de produire un joli son avec beaucoup d'archet.

Quels sont les paramètres supplémentaires apportés par la main gauche ? Pour commencer, la première note implique une position élevée, je dois donc démarrer très près du chevalet puis m'en éloigner quelque peu. Cela signifie que l'archet doit revenir un peu vers l'arrière.

• *crescendo – decrescendo*

Les variations dynamiques peuvent être obtenues de différentes manières. Je peux modifier le point de contact, la vitesse et le poids de l'archet. Généralement, ces trois paramètres influent simultanément.

Comme je souhaite ici donner de la légèreté au *piano* et commence déjà avec beaucoup d'archet, je dois modifier le point de contact et le poids de l'archet pour le *crescendo*. Cela signifie que je dois me déplacer en direction du chevalet en donnant davantage de poids au bras. Et inversement pour le *decrescendo*. Afin de ne pas produire de sons parasites en changeant de point de contact, je déplace l'archet non pas parallèlement au chevalet, mais légèrement en biais. C'est-à-dire que pour me déplacer vers lui, je dois tirer vers l'avant et pousser vers l'arrière, et inversement pour revenir en direction de la touche. Ici, je voudrais effectuer un *crescendo* plus particulièrement sur le poussé, en poussant vers l'intérieur. De ce fait, je me rapproche du chevalet pour obtenir davantage de son et jouer dans les positions hautes. Pour le *decrescendo*, je déplace également l'archet légèrement en biais afin de m'éloigner à nouveau du chevalet.

Coups d'archet :

• *legato*

Pour un beau *legato*, j'ai besoin d'une vitesse d'archet régulière. Là encore, il faut anticiper. Combien d'archet ai-je à disposition pour chaque note afin que mon son ne soit pas « maigrichon » ?

Ici, je dois diviser l'archet en trois parties égales. Cela signifie que l'archet devra immédiatement être plus lent que dans la mesure précédente et joué directement au chevalet. Le poids de l'archet sera réduit progressivement pour réaliser le *decrescendo*.

• *portato*

Pour le *portato*, il est important que l'archet ne s'arrête pas. Chaque son est formé séparément grâce aux variations de poids et de vitesse de l'archet, comme dans un petit mouvement de pendule.

Ici je voudrais donner une direction au 3e temps, c'est à dire que la première note aura moins d'archet que la deuxième et que la troisième note est celle qui en aura le plus.

• « Sons de cloches »

Les sons de cloches entrent en vibration puis s'éteignent comme le mouvement d'un pendule. Si j'utilise beaucoup d'archet, il en résulte une certaine légèreté ou un effet d'animation que je voudrais obtenir dans la partie centrale dansante.

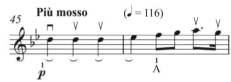

• Densité des changements de cordes

Afin d'obtenir la densité requise dans les changements de cordes, je dois me rapprocher lentement de la corde suivante, sans à coup. Pour cela, je dois apprendre à déterminer le moment où commencer le mouvement afin d'arriver à temps sur la nouvelle corde.

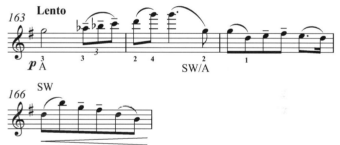

• Le son dans les positions hautes

Plus je monte dans les positions, plus l'archet doit se mouvoir vers le chevalet. Il est également utile ici de chercher la répartition d'archet adéquate et de la travailler sur une seule note. Les positions hautes sur la corde de *mi* nécessitent de bien doser le poids de l'archet afin de ne pas faire « grincer » le son.

Exercice préparatoire :

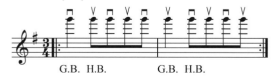

B. Exigences techniques pour la main gauche

La main gauche est elle aussi très sollicitée afin de donner toutes ses couleurs à l'interprétation de cette pièce et utiliser les qualités sonores spécifiques des différentes cordes. Cela implique notamment de nombreux changements de positions et des extensions. Il est également possible de faire parfois des *glissandi*. Du fait de nombreuses variations harmoniques et des changements de tonalité, l'intonation constitue ici un défi. Il est important de toujours savoir dans quelle position on se trouve : où sont mes demi-tons, quels sont les doigts qui sont rapprochés, ceux qui sont éloignés ?
En outre, l'utilisation d'un vibrato variable est essentielle.

Cette pièce nécessitant toutes sortes de changements de positions, je voudrais ici ne parler que de la différence entre un changement complet de position et la technique de l'extension, en l'illustrant d'exemples. Ce sont là les sources d'erreurs les plus fréquentes.
Les personnes souhaitant approfondir le sujet des changements de positions se reporteront à l'ouvrage suivant : *Systematische Violintechnik* (Schott ED 21162–21164). Je le leur recommande.

Un changement de position signifie que toute la main se déplace dans une nouvelle position. Ce processus est perceptible dans le *legato*. L'extension permet de n'étirer qu'un seul doigt dans la nouvelle position, vers le haut ou vers le bas, et le cas échéant, d'adopter ensuite la nouvelle position avec la main entière lors de l'étape suivante. Cela permet d'éviter de faire entendre des sons parasites. Le choix du mouvement est souvent déterminé par des critères d'ordre musical, en fonction de ce que l'on veut entendre. (Parfois, il est également nécessaire de tenir compte de ses propres capacités liées à la taille de sa main). Quoi qu'il en soit, il est important d'être au clair par rapport à la différence de mouvement et de décider lequel on veut exécuter pour une bonne précision et une meilleure intonation.

La technique de l'extension joue un grand rôle dans ce morceau, mais elle est rarement utilisée et travaillée de manière systématique. C'est pourquoi je voudrais présenter cette technique et l'expliquer ici à l'aide de deux exemples et des exercices préparatoires correspondants.

Exemple 1 : Extension vers le haut

Exercice préparatoire :

Exemple 2 : Extension vers le bas

Exercice préparatoire :

Dans ces deux exercices, la main conserve sa position initiale.

Annette Seyfried
Traduction Michaëla Rubi